MUSIC
FESTIVALS

 AN ESSENTIAL

pocket guide

★ TO SURVIVING ★

 in STYLE

D0569952

MUSIC FESTIVALS

Research by Sophie Martin

Summersdale Publishers Ltd
46 West Street
Chichester
West Sussex
PO19 1RP
UK

www.summersdale.com

Printed and bound in Malta

ISBN: 978-1-84953-701-8

Substantial discounts on bulk quantities of Summersdale books are available to corporations, professional associations and other organisations. For details contact general enquiries: telephone: +44 (0) 1243 771107, fax: +44 (0) 1243 786300 or email: enquiries@summersdale.com.

INTRODUCTION

You've been starved of the festival life for too long and the symptoms are getting considerably worse. No longer can you bear the humdrum of eating your five a day, having a regular sleeping pattern and using a toilet with a lid. But now you don't have to camp out in your back garden because it's time to stop pretending and start preparing for the biggest event in your calendar.

Whether you are getting ready for your first or your one hundred and first festival, this pocket-size book will be your go-to before and during your festival experience, packed with information and advice including festival hacks, DIY ideas and money-saving tips that'll have you looking and feeling like a festival aficionado. So dig out your wellies and stop waiting around because it's time to get your festival freak on!

THE TRANSPORT TICKET

You've just raided the entire contents of your piggy bank for your festival ticket and you still need to pay for transport. But although you'll have to meet the cost of the festival, you don't have to sell your arm and leg to get there.

First of all, meet up with the people you're going with to discuss your options well in advance, so that you're not organising your transport in a blind panic the day before you leave. This could also help you get better deals if you decide to use public transport.

If you know other people who aren't in your group but are going – people you don't absolutely abhor – look into sharing a private coach or minibus. Most festivals allow you to park your private coach or minibus on-site, as long as you contact them ahead of time to give details on the number of people attending, the date of arrival and the size of your vehicle – but do check with them first before booking anything.

If you're only travelling a short distance, or travelling lightly, it might be worth going by train (a lot of festivals advise this option). Go off-peak to make sure you get the best deal, and if you know what time train you want to catch both ways, select the super off-peak option, which gives you an even bigger discount. When you arrive at your destination, there are typically shuttle buses organised by the festival to take you to the site. Information on the shuttle-bus timetables are usually available on the respective festival website.

Another way to save money, and reduce your carbon footprint at the same time, is to go by coach. Other benefits of travelling by coach are that you are taken directly to the festival site and you can just sit back and enjoy yourself whilst someone else does the driving – this is a godsend, particularly on the way back from the festival. Nowadays, many festivals collaborate with coach companies and offer great deals to festival-goers from a number of different pick-up locations. To find out if the festival you are going to offers this package and where the pick-up locations are, visit the festival website, which will redirect you to the coach company's website for additional information.

Another option for going easy on the spending is to car share. Try gocarshare.com, which enables you to search for people in your area who are car sharing via Facebook. Liftshare.com and blablacar.com will also put you in touch with other members on their websites who are looking at taking/going with other people.

If you are travelling abroad to a festival, book your flight tickets well in advance to secure a seat, and organise your transfer before you get there to make your travelling less stressful once you arrive in the new country.

If you are thinking about taking a car and you are the designated driver, think this through carefully before you agree to it. On the way there, the drive will be pleasant enough, but on returning home you'll be tired and maybe still under the influence without even knowing it, which makes the chances of having an accident or getting into trouble with the police much higher. Also be aware that at most festivals you will experience delays getting out of the site at peak times – so there's no point rushing to get home on the last day, as that extra time could help you work any substances out of your system so that you're safe to drive.

★ FASHION ME FESTIVAL ★

STEALTH BELT

While the festival toffs will be brandishing their royal red notes, you, oh sensible one, have the brains to know that this sort of behaviour could be the harbinger of bad things to come. To help you feel completely secure about the money you carry on you, you need a stealth belt – or, in other words, a makeshift bum bag you wear on the inside of your trousers, shorts or skirt. Here's how to make one from scratch:

What you need: plain fabric coin purse, an old pair of jeans, shorts or T-shirt, plastic Ladderloc buckle, strong glue, thread and needle.

1 Find or buy a fabric coin purse. A plain purse with no embellishments is recommended; you don't want to go home with phantom scratch marks on your groin.

Take a strip of material, cut from an old piece of clothing you no longer wear, that is approximately 25 mm wide and one and a half times the size of your waist.

 Align the purse to the strip of material so that one end is longer than the other and sew the material securely onto one side of the purse.

 Then take a plastic Ladderloc buckle – the type with three or four bars, usually found on rucksacks – and thread the shorter side of material through the buckle so you make a small loop. Glue the material together and sew across the joining point for extra strength.

 When you want to wear your stealth belt, wrap it around your tummy, feed the longer strip of material through the buckle (double it up as an extra precaution), stash the requisite money in the purse and put on your bottom half of clothing. Freely dance, jump and jive without anyone knowing you have any money on you at all!

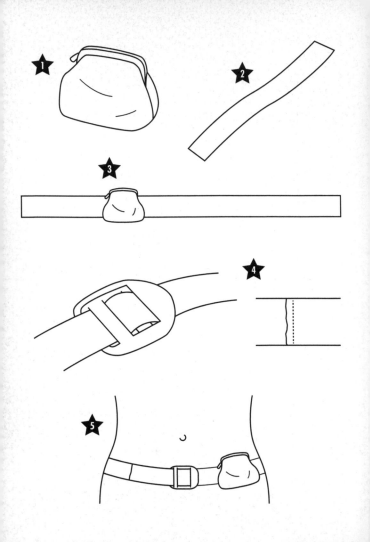

THE ONLY TRUTH IS MUSIC.

★ Jack Kerouac ★

≈ FESTIVAL FAUX PAS ≈

VIDEO KILLED THE FESTIVAL FUN

Don't take videos of your favourite acts. As well as getting stern looks from the people around you as you block their view with your arm stuck in the air, you'll miss out on seeing them live. And let's face it, no matter how many megapixels your phone has, it will never beat the cameras used to broadcast on TV. If you want to relive your memories then get someone you know who isn't going to record it at home, or, if the festival you're attending isn't being broadcast, go on YouTube and watch some other sucker's video. Put your phone in your pocket, keep it there and experience the spectacle with your own eyes.

TOP TIP

CONFISCATION OPERATION

At every festival I know of, there are certain items that aren't allowed on-site. It's pretty obvious to most that you aren't allowed to take items such as flares and fireworks, but time and time again people do. Still, there are less obvious things that aren't permitted, such as umbrellas, and you don't want to have something that you paid for taken away if you can help it. Here's a list of the no-no items that seem to be most common among festivals:

★ Air horns

★ Animals

★ Audio recorders

★ Chinese lanterns

★ Excessive amounts of alcohol, cigarettes or food

MUSIC FESTIVALS

★ Fireworks

★ Flares

★ Generators

★ Glass bottles, jars and containers

★ Illegal substances

★ Items for unauthorised trading

★ Items with unauthorised logos (fake merchandise)

★ Items that could be considered for use as a weapon

★ Megaphones

★ Nitrous oxide

★ Portable laser equipment and pens

★ Sound systems

★ Spray cans

★ Umbrellas

★ Unauthorised professional film or video equipment

Most festival websites will provide a list of what you aren't allowed to bring, so check that first before you start packing.

WHEN I HEAR MUSIC, I FEAR NO DANGER.

I AM INVULNERABLE. *I see no foe.*

I AM RELATED TO THE EARLIEST TIMES, **AND TO THE LATEST.**

★ *Henry David Thoreau* ★

≈ FESTIVAL FAUX PAS ≈

WHAT NOT TO WEAR...

Playsuits and jumpsuits seem like the perfect outfits to take to a festival. They are stylish, light to wear and don't take up much room in your luggage. But don't be lured by their seemingly good functionality because you'll soon be cursing once you break the seal. It's bad enough being in a Portaloo, let alone being naked in one. As well as concentrating on where to aim and what not to touch, you will also have to secure the outfit with one hand to spare it from falling to its stinky fate on the ground.

If you don't take heed of this tip, make sure you pay attention to this: take a suit that hasn't got strings, ties or belts that are long enough to inadvertently dunk into the toilet's swampy waters – you really don't want to be tying up loo-soaked strings.

WORST FESTIVAL MOMENT

After much deliberation over whether this should appear as a worst or best festival moment, I decided out of the goodness of my heart that no one deserves what happened at the 2000 Reading Festival, not even the 'Ooh Stick You' duo Daphne and Celeste. Therefore, I present to you one of the worst moments in festival history (for them at least): while performing the one – some say only – song that made them super-famous, Daphne and Celeste had to endure a painful 3 minutes of being pummelled by airborne bottles and God knows what else. Luckily they stayed unbelievably composed throughout the entire song and were still smiling in their post-performance interview. But it's not just Daphne and Celeste who have had to tolerate this bottle-throwing frenzy; Meat Loaf, My Chemical Romance and 50 Cent have all been subjected to it, while Green Day are remembered for victoriously defending their place on stage by throwing the clumps of mud and grass that had been thrown at them back at the audience, creating a huge mud fight.

DID YOU KNOW?

During a Glastonbury Festival weekend, 3 million gallons of water are consumed, 2,500 toilets are used and 800,000 million gallons of human waste are collected.

TOP TIP

TEN CAMPERS, ONE TENT

Your tent will be your trusty companion during your festival stay – it will be your protection when the heavens open, your lullaby when your eyes can't stay open any longer and your chill-out zone when things get too much. But enough already, because if you don't choose your tent correctly, then it will be your nemesis.

Tents are measured in berths, which refers to the amount of people and luggage they can hold. A lot of people make the mistake of choosing a berth size just big enough for the number of people who will be using the tent but often forget that each person will be carrying at least one rucksack, not to mention carrier bags, food coolers and containers, etc.

If you are sleeping in a tent with one other person, it is usually recommended that you buy a tent with a berth of four; if there are three of you, then a five-berth tent is advisable. However, if you know that your luggage amounts to a week's worth of clothing and the kitchen sink it's a safe bet to choose the next berth up from what's recommended. You don't want to end up having to make the choice of whether it's you or the luggage that sleeps outside.

★ FESTIVAL HACK ★

It's a nightmare when you're trying to get some sleep and all you can feel is the lumps and bumps of the ground beneath you. Try this hack for a comfier time camping.

Buy some interlocking foam floor tiles – the ones that are used in children's nurseries – or a couple of yoga mats. Once you've pitched your tent, put them down on the base of the tent for extra padding. Happy comfy camping!

≈ FESTIVAL FAUX PAS ≈

DRIP, DRIP, DRIPPING ON SOMEONE'S TENT DOOR

Do unto others as you would have them do to you and don't go urinating on someone else's tent. OK, you might be desperate and the victim's tent is the nearest thing around to relieve yourself on, or you might have your friends egging you on to do it as a dare, but think about the poor person/ people who will have to wake to the sound of a fountain against their head. A note of advice: thinkle before you sprinkle.

AFTER SILENCE,

THAT WHICH COMES

NEAREST TO

expressing the inexpressible

IS MUSIC.

★ *Aldous Huxley* ★

TOP TIP

ELECTRIC NIGHTS

As technology is ever-expanding, so is the quantity of gadgets you carry with you on a daily basis. No matter how naked you feel without certain items, strip yourself of the unnecessary ones when you pack for the festival and try going back to basics – you'll be having such a good time that you'll forget about them anyway. However, if you can't go without for one weekend, try only taking the items below:

★ Phone
★ Portable phone charger
★ LED light keyring (for when you're trying to find your way back to the tent at night)
★ Solar shower (if you're not willing to rough it)

If you're finding it difficult to resist slipping that Coolpix camera into your bag, you won't be hung, drawn and quartered if you do, but you'll be shooting yourself in the foot if you think the following items are going to heighten your festival experience:

★ eReaders – the last thing you'll want to do is read when you've had four hours' sleep and feel like you're in a coma from all the booze.

★ iPads, including iPad minis – tourists with iPads constantly in their hands are irritating enough, let alone festival tourists in the middle of a crowd trying to film every single second of every performance, regardless of whether they actually like the band.

★ Any device that depends on WiFi only – most festivals do not have WiFi and the few that do can only provide a limited service that reaches people standing no more than ten metres away. The probability that you will pitch your tent in that proximity is next to nil and it's very unlikely that you will fancy standing around in one tiny area of the festival when there's so much more to explore.

★ Bluetooth headset – even disregarding the question of WiFi, you shouldn't at any time be wearing one of these full stop.

DID YOU KNOW?

Roskilde Festival in Denmark gives its attendees the chance to win tickets for the following year's festival by hosting a naked race. The first man and first woman to run, bounce and swing their way to the finish line are the winners. When the festival organisers conducted a survey about the race, 96 per cent of those surveyed said they were more interested in studying the racers' body parts than in finding out who the winners were.

★ FASHION ME FESTIVAL ★

GLITZY GLASSES

Glam up your standard festival outfit with some glitzy glasses and wear them from sunrise to sunset.

What you need: Sunglasses, colourful and glittery nail polishes, sunshine.

 Find an old pair of sunglasses.

 Buy or have a rummage for a funky-coloured nail polish.

 Apply one coat to the frame and leave to dry.

 Then, apply a second coat. If you really want to stand out from the crowd, use a glittery nail polish as a sealer.

 Voilà! Take them with you, pray for some sunshine and wear them with style – and, hopefully, sun in your eyes, or maybe even stars.

Next to music, BEER WAS BEST.

★ *Carson McCullers* ★

TOP TIP

GET ORGANISED

It's been months since you booked your festival ticket, so long ago that you aren't even sure whether it was a dream or reality. However, before you know it, time will creep up on you and you'll soon be making your way there. But before you arrive, it's worth getting together with your friends to come up with a vague plan of who wants to see which band and do what when, especially if it's one of the bigger festivals you are attending.

You don't have to turn into Sherlock Holmes about it and look into every last detail, but at the same time you don't want to be wandering around gormlessly while trying to decide which act you'd prefer to see – you probably won't get to see any of them at that rate. Get your hands on a timetable of the performances, jot down the must-sees on a piece of paper and take it with you. Or, if you are a part of the technologically advanced generation, you can always list the events you'd like to see on your phone, in your notes or calendar. Try not to be too ambitious with how much you think you can do; giving yourself some blank spaces will mean you have enough time for some spontaneous activities, or even for a power nap/chill-out sesh too.

I DO KNOW

THE EFFECT

that music still has on me -

I'M COMPLETELY VULNERABLE TO IT.

I'M SEDUCED BY IT.

★ *Debbie Harry* ★

≈ FESTIVAL FAUX PAS ≈

A LITTLE BIT OF MOANICA CAN GET OUT MY LIFE

Inside you can cry all you like about the limited bathroom facilities, the way the wind beats against the side of the tent when you are trying to sleep, and half the headliners being 'the worst bands IN THE WORLD', but make sure on the outside you hold it all together, because no one likes someone who incessantly moans.

TOP TIP

YOUR FIRST AID FOR FIRST AID

Beat the queue for the first-aid tent by being prepared with your own mini first-aid kit. This way you won't have to miss out on any of the acts you planned to see because you stapled your hand as a dare when you were drunk the night before. Here are some essentials to include:

★ An assortment of strong fabric plasters (waterproof plasters will slip off the minute you start to sweat)

★ Blister pads

★ Antiseptic wipes and cream

★ Antiseptic gloves

★ Gauze bandages

★ Safety pins

★ Pain relief tablets

★ Eye wash

★ Burn gel/cream

★ Prescription medicine, if necessary

★ Sun cream

DID YOU KNOW?

Fuji Rock Festival in Japan, surrounded by mountains and beautiful forests, has been named as the best festival for natural scenery.

★ FESTIVAL HACK ★

Water and food that hasn't gone off or become stagnant from the heat of the day is not just nice to have, it can be an essential, especially if you're on a budget and you don't want to pay out for expensive festie nourishment. To make sure you have plenty of both, thoroughly clean and refill 6-pint plastic milk bottles three-quarters full with water and freeze them. Before leaving for the festival, put them in a cool box alongside your food. Not only will these bumper ice-packs keep your food cooler for longer, as the ice melts you'll have cold water to hydrate yourself with.

ART IS THE BEST WAY to push a MOVEMENT.

★ Sini Anderson ★

BEST FESTIVAL MOMENT

Towering books lined up in a row, a magnificent butterfly majestically overlooking the crowds and a multi-coloured palace with a royal design. These are just some of the stages that Tomorrowland in Belgium boasts. If you're in a dilemma trying to decide which festival you want to go to, take a look at some of the photos – they might just be the deciding factor!

TOP TIP

SHOWER ME HAPPY

Even the most hygienic people have to come to terms with the lack of shower facilities at festivals, and most of the time they leave the festival fully embracing the dirt and smell they have managed to build up, only to have to go back to civilised society and be frowned upon by others. What I'm about to say may shock you, and you may be so put off that you actually put down this book and set it alight, but I fully encourage any festival goer to leave their 101 products at home. But if you are horrified by this prospect, then be savvy with your luggage space and organise with your friends to share toiletries, thus dramatically cutting the quantity you need to take.

~ FESTIVAL FAUX PAS ~

OUT OF PLACE

I LOVE fancy dress at a festival, especially when everyone's got the fancy dress memo. The costumes are imaginative, well-crafted and fun – that's until you spot a group of guys dancing like maniacs in their morphsuits. If you are thinking of parading in your morphsuits that you took to Gary's stag-do in 2001 or taking uniform from your school days that is now three sizes too small, think again and leave them at home. You'd be better off wearing normal clothes – that's how unoriginal they are.

★ FESTIVAL HACK ★

In my opinion, as you may have figured by now, toiletries are a royal pain in the backside. When you have only limited space, you don't want your luxury items, such as toothpaste and eau de toilette, taking up half of it. However, by the second day of the festival, when your breath is as rough as the festival toilets, you may need a hygiene pick-me-up to feel slightly more human again. These luxury items, as I call them, don't have to be sacrificed if you use this handy hack:

1 Take a jumbo straw – the wider the better – and cut it into small parts, depending on how many luxury products you want take and how much you think you'll need of each product.

Pinch one of the open ends of the straw and hold a flame by the pinched area so that the plastic melts and acts as a glue, sticking the two edges together. But be careful, as you don't want to glue your fingers to the plastic too, or end up in the casualty department with burns.

 Wait for the plastic to cool, then decant one use of the liquid, whether it's your toothpaste or perfume or aftershave, into the straw container, leaving a 2-cm gap at the top.

 Then pinch the top edges of the straw together and hold a flame by them to seal the straw completely. Hold the straw upright until the plastic at the top cools.

 Make as many as you'll need for a weekend. All you have to do when you come to use them is cut one of the seals with some nail scissors. Feeling fresh (or fresher than you were) and being lightly packed at a festival was never easier!

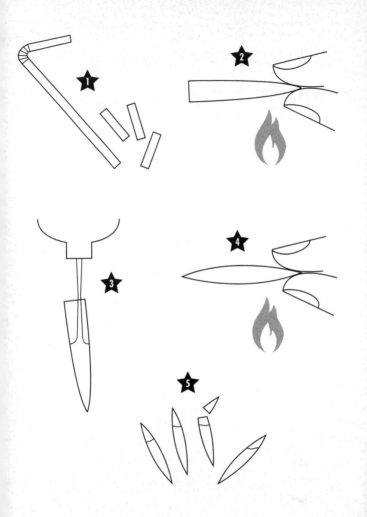

WITHOUT MUSIC
TO DECORATE IT,
time is just a bunch of
BORING PRODUCTION
DEADLINES
OR DATES BY WHICH BILLS
MUST BE PAID.

★ *Frank Zappa* ★

DID YOU KNOW?

The Coachella Festival, California, is located in the Colorado Desert. Temperatures have ranged from 41 degrees to 107 degrees Fahrenheit. Being quite the opposite of a UK summer festival, you might want to think about going if you fancy getting a summer holiday out of it too, but do be prepared!

TOP TIP

Hot temperatures, crowded spaces and long hours dancing to your favourite bands – that's what a festival is all about (well, the heat is the biggest variable if you're planning a UK festival). To make sure you don't overheat like a car engine, follow these top tips on how to stay well ventilated:

In the summer, avoid black at all costs, even if you are a die-hard goth. The colour will absorb the heat and leave you feeling like a radiator. The opposite colour to black that will reflect heat the most is white. If you don't like white, go for pale colours instead, as they will have more or less the same effect.

Wear natural fabrics, such as wool, cotton or linen. These fabrics help increase the airflow to your skin.

Loose-fitting or floaty outfits will help your skin stay cooler. Tight-fitting clothes retain sweat for longer and by the time you've finished dancing to one song you'll feel like you've just had your first festival (sweat) shower.

If I ever had the chance to appear on *Dragons' Den*, I'd put my money where my mouth is with non-stick sunscreen for scalps. But the chances of that happening are slim and the reason why I always take a hat with me. A short-brimmed straw hat will help prevent you looking like you have a severe case of dandruff the next day. But if you want something that will protect your face too, I suggest taking a mid-brimmed or floppy hat, although some may find the floppy hat too distracting when you're craning your neck to see a band and all you can see is straw. Another more practical option that will give you more room in your luggage is a headscarf.

D is for Denim and for Danger too. If you think you can survive a long weekend without your trusty jeans, then I suggest you do just that. As well as being a heat insulator and a burden to your dancing legs, they take up essential luggage space, and when it rains there's nothing worse than having a soggy bottom and heavy legs for the rest of the day.

Every night I play AS IF MY LIFE DEPENDS ON IT.

★ *Billie Joe Armstrong* ★

FASHION ME FESTIVAL

FOR-THE-WIN WELLIES

We've all seen what a wet festival can be like. And if you're going to a festival based in the UK then it's very likely that you will experience sludge, slime and squalor. While other festival goers will be donning the over-priced wellies that share the name given to elite shooting types, you can fashion some rough-and-ready wellies that are as effective and 99 per cent cheaper. Here's how to make them:

What you need: 4–6 plastic bags (without holes), duct tape, a small pair of scissors.

 Stash a roll of duct tape and lots of plastic bags in your luggage. Don't worry about these taking up lots of space, their form is much more malleable than the stiff, long-necked wellies that your friends are trying to stuff into their already over-packed bags.

 Hope for the rain to stay away.

Watch the clouds multiply and the rain crash down. Go back to the tent.

 With your shoes still on (make sure they aren't your two-day-old Vans), wrap a plastic bag around each foot and tie the handles firmly in a knot, though not so tight that you cut off your circulation.

 With the scissors, make holes in two more plastic bags big enough to slide your feet through. Put them round each leg so that they slightly overlap the other bags and tie the handles in a knot to secure them around your legs.

 Depending on how tall you are – I'm very short – you may have to repeat step 5 once more further up your calves.

 Then here comes the duct tape – the more colourful and designed, the better. Wind the duct tape round each leg starting at your toes and finishing where the plastic bags meet your flesh or clothes. Remember to circle the duct tape two to three times where the two plastic bags meet and where the makeshift wellie ends for extra waterproof protection.

Splash in the swamp that is forming underneath your feet and embrace the opportunity to be dancing in the rain. Let's face it, soon enough you'll be cursing the weather as you try to navigate the pavements back home with a broken umbrella and the wind and rain slapping against your face.

WORST FESTIVAL MOMENT

Unlike Daphne and Celeste, who handled their bottle attack extremely calmly, this cannot be said for grime artist Dizzee Rascal. At the 2010 Big Day Out in Sydney, Dizzee took a blow to the head in the shape of a deodorant can. But instead of standing up tall, he flew into the audience, only to be restrained by security. If I could have comforted Dizzee after the tormenting incident I would have reassured him that the culprit was no more than just a rascal.

TOP TIP

If you are loath to lug heavy bags but would prefer that to facing a common toilet terror that could be prevented, then take the weight on the chin (not literally) and get pumping iron in preparation for transporting toilet roll, and lots of it. Some festivals will ensure that toilet roll is provided, others will not, but either way, by the second day, toilet roll is the festival equivalent of the Holy Grail. Once you've safely delivered the toilet roll to where you're going to be staying, don't just forget about it and leave it in the corner of your tent under your dirty pants – make sure that you have liberal amounts with you at all times before you leave your living area. The last thing you want is to be caught out in a Portaloo with nothing but a clean hand (for now) and a white outfit.

MUSIC... CAN NAME THE UNNAMEABLE AND COMMUNICATE THE UNKNOWABLE.

★ *Leonard Bernstein* ★

≋ FESTIVAL FAUX PAS ≋

NO AGGRO, NO CRY

At some point when you're watching a set, there will be someone trying to squeeze through a throng of people to get out of the crowd. Instead of huffing, tsking and reprimanding them under your breath, make way to let them through. There'll be a hundred more people making rude gestures, so be the better person – it's not the biggest deal in the world.

TOP TIP

Baby wipes, baby wipes, baby wipes, baby wipes, baby wipes, baby wipes, baby wipes, baby wipes, baby wipes, baby wipes – you can never have enough baby wipes at a festival.

DID YOU KNOW?

The Woodstock Festival of 1969 wasn't actually held in Woodstock. Because the locations in Woodstock itself weren't suitable, they settled for an industrial site near Middletown, New York instead.

★ FESTIVAL HACK ★

Sick of holding a torch or your phone when you are trying to find something in your tent at night? Remember to pack a large water bottle and a head lamp with an elastic attachment. When it gets dark, secure the headlamp to the water bottle using its strap, so the light is facing inwards, and voilà you have yourself your own free-standing lamp that illuminates the whole tent, not just where you are facing.

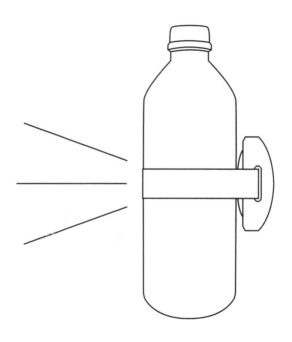

IF I CAN'T DANCE TO IT, it's not my ▲ REVOLUTION.

★ *Emma Goldman* ★

TOP TIP

FOOD FOR THOUGHT

Unfortunately, unlike a holiday in a country brimming with exotic tastes and delicious delicacies, the food of some festivals is a menu of little variation and big price tags. If you want to keep your cash for a meal more memorable than a mouthful of grease, first check whether the festival you are attending permits you to bring food into the venue and, if it does, buy some supplies before setting off. Food that is durable and long-lasting, and that can be eaten with no fuss is what you need to look for when rummaging the aisles of the supermarket. Here's a list of recommended foods to take for snacking and breakfasting on:

THE GOOD
(if you're feeling a little worse for wear and need to beat the hangover):

★ Granola bars

★ Dried fruit

★ Fresh fruit (but only the hardy stuff, such as apples, pears and oranges)

★ Peanut butter or jam

★ Bread, rolls or bagels (or all three)

★ Crackers

★ Pre-made salads (including rice and potato salads to maintain your energy levels)

★ Hummus and carrots

★ Cereal (if you like eating it dry)

★ Nuts

THE BAD

(if you're feeling a little worse for wear and need to think that you're beating the hangover but are in fact only causing a placebo effect):

★ Crisps

★ Chocolate (remember to keep it cool, as sweaty chocolate is definitely not cool)

★ Sausage rolls, pies and pasties

★ Sugary sweets

★ Cold pizza (cooked the day before)

★ The mighty Pot Noodle

★ Flapjacks

FASHION ME FESTIVAL

FASHION YOUR BODY

Festival outfits are fun to plan with your friends, but why stop at the clothes when you can fashion your face too? Come to the festival equipped with some or all of the following face/body-paint products:

★ Basic face/body paints

★ Neon face/body paints

★ Metallic face/body paints

★ Glitter gels

★ Brushes to apply face/body paint

★ Make-up remover/wipes (you don't want to look like something out of a horror film the day after)

If you're like me, you will need some creative guidance before you put the brush to yours or your friend's skin. Here are some of the funkier styles and patterns I've learned from trial and error – once I saw my reflection and thought I had turned into a bona fide avatar:

The Geometric

An easy one to get right and recommended for L-plate face-painters. Design includes dots, lines, linking circles and cool angular patterns. The patterns you create should resemble tribal patterns. Best parts of the body to apply this style to are wrists, ankles, hands, feet and the strip of your face level with your eyes. Use metallic paints to create an authentic tribal look.

The Glitter

Shimmer and sparkle,
And almost everything nice
That's what festival-goers are made of.

Join the glitterati and put the pizazz into your festival experience. Add glitter in a band across your eyes and the bridge of your nose for a simple but stylish look. But beware, it's easy to get carried away and you could end up looking like an alien or one of the vampires from *Twilight*. To avoid this humiliation, never mix your glitter colours and never apply the glitter to more than one-fifth of your face. Less is definitely more.

The Floral

This one's to flower power in all its flowery glory. Never has the flower gone out of fashion at festivals, which is why I always fall back on it if feeling doubtful about the latest (ridiculous) trends.

This face art (and I call it art because it requires a certain level of artistry) can be perfected with some practice beforehand. For a simpler pattern, paint a line of daisies under your eyes or, for a more innovative approach, you could get all deconstructive and freestyle the petals, leaves and stamen. (Although don't blame me if people then strike up conversations about Jacques Derrida and the form of semiotic analysis with you.) Use pastel-coloured paints to complement this style.

The Simplistic

If you've tried all the above and can almost certainly say that you have the artistic ability of a baked bean, this style may be the one for you. You don't have to be Picasso to make your face look like a masterpiece.

Try adding two lines shaped like arrows underneath one eye or painting zigzags across your forehead and cheekbones. Because this style lends itself to simplicity, make it stand out by using neon-coloured paints.

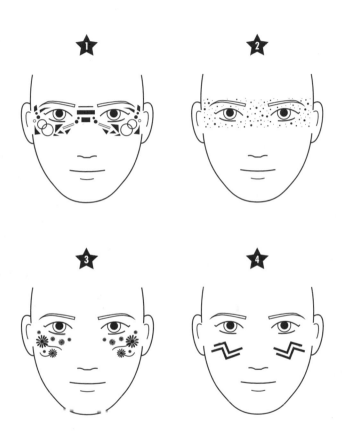

I'm not saying I'm gonna
CHANGE THE WORLD,
but... I will spark
THE BRAIN
THAT WILL CHANGE
THE WORLD.

★ *Tupac Shakur* ★

TOP TIP

SUPERMARKET SWEEP, SUPERMARKET STOP

When you have limited time and you're under pressure to scour the supermarket aisles for food that you need to survive on, sometimes it can be easy to pick up everything you see. This sort of behaviour usually ends up with you having to carry heavy bags of food that you are certain will be wasted, therefore becoming a burden on both your wallet and your muscles. To avoid this, be realistic about how much of the shop-bought food you and your friends will eat and how much will, in fact, be supplanted by the flirty burger that has been eyeing you up since you arrived. All it takes is one hangover and *bam*, your defences are down.

You will need to check before you go, but some festivals have supermarkets on-site where you can stock up on food. They will be more expensive than your local Lidl but compared with the festival's food stalls, it'll hardly make a mark on your limited budget.

DID YOU KNOW?

Pohoda Festival in Slovakia takes after its name, meaning 'well-being', as festival attendees can kick off their shoes and relax in huge chill-out tents or unwind from the buzz of the campsite with a holistic treatment or massage.

BEST FESTIVAL MOMENT

On 25 June 2009 Michael Jackson, the King of Pop, died. What better way to pay homage to him than by creating an ensemble movement of what he did best? At the 2009 Fusion Festival in Germany hundreds of people got together and moonwalked back and forth. The crowd grew bigger and the moonwalking got progressively worse, but what a great send-off for a man whose immense contribution to the music industry has influenced so many artists.

≈ FESTIVAL FAUX PAS ≈

JACKIE BIG HEELS

The thought of taking heels to a festival shouldn't even cross your mind. First, you're not there to parade your new 6-inchers because – honestly – no one cares. Second, it's hard enough walking on slabbed pavement in the city without getting your heel caught in the gap, let alone squelching through mud all day only to have to go back to the tent early to change them because the pain is too much to bear.

MUSIC GIVES A SOUL

TO THE UNIVERSE,

WINGS TO THE MIND,

flight to the imagination

AND LIFE TO ⛺

EVERYTHING.

★ *Plato* ★

TOP TIP

NOT CHOOSING THE WRONG SPOT

You've arrived early at your destination – because you are sensible – but now you're confounded by the choice of where to pitch up. Although it's difficult to say definitively where the best spots to lay claim to are – there are too many festivals and landscapes to give you that sort of conclusive answer – here are a few tips on where not to choose:

First is an obvious one, but not so obvious that people continually feel the need to make the mistake and the reason why it's here in black and white. Don't camp near any stage – whether big, small, round, square or the one where your all-time favourite band will be performing – or right next to a path that leads to one of the main stages. If you do, you'll soon find out why it was a mistake. As well as being the most concentrated areas of people, they are the most concentrated areas of drunken (and otherwise intoxicated) people. So if at 3.30 in the morning you experience your tent collapse from the weight of a kebab-munching, beer-slurping giant falling against it, no one but yourself is to blame.

You spot another area well away from the stages, positioned between the Portaloos and the burger van. It's a place of serene quiet now, but when the evening comes it'll soon metamorphose into something that smells permanently like your local sewage plant – and I'm just talking about the food. Another place you should also avoid pitching your tent on or around is what looks like a popular walkway.

You've listened to the advice and have stayed well away from the two areas just mentioned. However, all this caution has made you suspicious of even the most alluring spots.

You end up travelling to the most discreet part of the campsite, away from the raucous of the other campers, protected by a hill. You pitch your tent and start some food on the disposable BBQ. And then the first drops of rain begin to fall. In minutes the rain begins its course down the hill, a collective army of water droplets, making their attack from the upper ground. What seemed like the perfect pitching ground has resulted in a waterlogged tent and some soggy burgers. Beware of hillsides, especially if you are festivalling in the wetter climates of the UK.

After all this information of places to avoid, you may be wondering whether you should just burn your festival ticket and not bother going at all. But don't pick up that lighter just yet, as there is some good news ahead. When you've got away from the hills, the big stages and main paths, all you will see is rolling fields. There's a lot of good space to choose from if you are an early bird, so take your pick.

★ FESTIVAL HACK ★

Ticks can't hop, jump, fly, swim or make noises. But they do have one hell of a grip when they bite, and once they have their hold on you they are nasty to remove. But you don't even need to think about removing them when you use this tick-repellent hack that will stop them coming near you in the first place.

Put one part tea tree oil and two parts water into a spray bottle. Spray it onto your clothes, shoes and tent to create a force field against the ticks.

MUSIC MAKES ME
HIGH ONSTAGE,
IT'S ALMOST LIKE BEING
ADDICTED TO MUSIC.

★ *Jimi Hendrix* ★

MARKING THE SPOT

Once you've pitched your tent, you'll be wanting a 5-minute break to get your sanity back – well, if you're like me you will anyway. But your work is not done yet, so take a few deep breaths (or swigs of beer) and get back up on your feet.

Before others start congregating nearby, make sure you signal to them that the space around your tent is yours too. Like the cat does to your front-door area but without the urinating part, mark your territory. Do this by putting down blankets and setting up pop-up chairs, or whatever you can get your hands on, in the area around your tent(s). That way, when you go off to explore you won't have to come back to see that your entrance now backs onto someone else's.

★ FASHION ME FESTIVAL ★

WASHER AND RIBBON NECKLACE

Instead of paying big bucks for a cheap necklace from a high street shop, why not pay cheap change for cheap materials and make your own necklace – makes sense, doesn't it?

What you need: metal washers (approx. 25–30, depending on how long you want your necklace to be) and grosgrain ribbon (approx. 36 in, but again it depends how long you want the necklace to be).

 Thread the ribbon through one of the washers, leaving enough space at one end of the ribbon to tie the necklace when finished.

 Using the part of the ribbon you threaded through the washer, thread it through another washer, but this time thread it down.

⭐ **3** Hold the second washer in the air and thread the ribbon down through the first washer.

⭐ **4** Pull the ribbon tight, so the second washer is lying flat on top of the first washer.

⭐ **5** Thread the ribbon back up through the second washer, then repeat steps 2 to 5 until there is an equal amount of ribbon at both ends.

⭐ **6** All that's left to do now is tie the ends of the ribbon in a knot and trim off any excess ribbon.

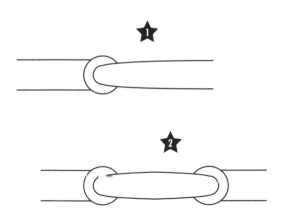

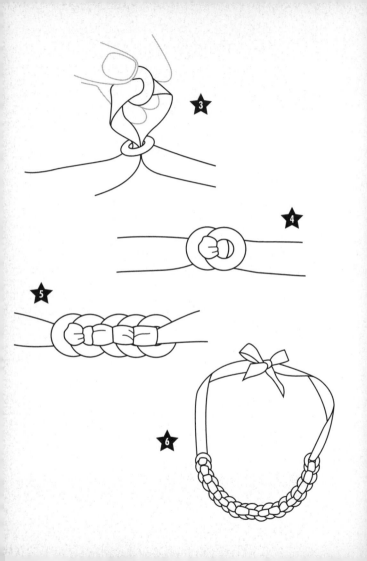

When you're on stage,
THE REAL WORLD
JUST DROPS AWAY
FOR THAT TIME.
IT'S PRETTY
INTENSE.

★ *Robert Smith* ★

TOP TIP

A FIELD AND TENT KINDA LANDSCAPE

The scenery isn't varied, and with the addition of a sea of tents of similar size, shape and colour it's easy to get confused as to where you pitched yours – so you need to make sure that you'll be able to get back to it at the end of the day, with a fuzzy head and a fatigued body. With this in mind, try to choose a spot that is next to or near a memorable landmark. Perhaps there's a towering or striking tree, a corner of a field or a colourful stall that sells something specific nearby.

To help you trace your tracks back to where you're staying, video yourself walking either to or from your tent to a place that's easy to spot. Focus on the landmarks you pass. If you're someone who's super-forgetful and doesn't mind getting strange looks, it might even be worth doing a running commentary while you're making the video to help prompt you.

DID YOU KNOW?

Over the duration of four major UK festivals, on average over 8.2 million metres of toilet paper are used. When every UK festival is included, an estimated 15 million metres of toilet paper are used by attendees and staff every year. That's about 5,000 miles, or the distance from London to Rome in festival toilet paper.

MUSIC WAS

MY REFUGE.

I could crawl into the space

BETWEEN THE NOTES

and curl my back to

LONELINESS.

★ *Maya Angelou* ★

≈ FESTIVAL FAUX PAS ≈

WE'RE ALL GOING ON A SUITCASE HOLIDAY

Festivals are synonymous with mud, so it wouldn't be the greatest idea you've ever had to take a wheelie suitcase with you. If it's been raining the wheels are bound to collect mud and get stuck, resulting in you having to carry it the rest of the way to the campsite. Even if you are lucky and the terrain is dry, you're still going to be up against the lumps, bumps, rises and falls of the ground. Another reason to leave the suitcase at home is that even the dinkiest ones will take up a large proportion of your tent.

TOP TIP

MAKE FRIENDS, NOT ENEMIES

The worst thing you can acquire at a festival is an enemy. Especially an enemy who lives next door. Once you know who your neighbours are and you are sure that they are settled and not frantically running around like headless chickens trying to put their tent up before nightfall, take the time to go and see them to casually say hi. By no means do you have to try to become BFFs, but a quick greeting will show them that you don't want to cause or receive any hassle or trouble. By being pleasant to them now might work in your favour too if you end up embarrassing yourself by being too drunk that same night.

YOU LISTEN TO MUSIC
because you want

★ FASHION ME FESTIVAL ★

BEADY GONZALES

Tassel and bead yourself silly with this DIY idea that'll turn your plain and boring white T-shirt into a funky fashion statement.

What you need: different-coloured beads (different shapes and sizes optional), plain white T-shirt, scissors.

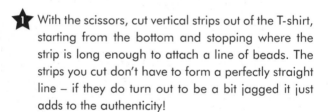

1 With the scissors, cut vertical strips out of the T-shirt, starting from the bottom and stopping where the strip is long enough to attach a line of beads. The strips you cut don't have to form a perfectly straight line – if they do turn out to be a bit jagged it just adds to the authenticity!

2 Once you have cut round the whole of the T-shirt, you are ready to add the beads. Take one of the strips and twist it. Then apply 3–5 beads onto the strip, tying a knot after so that they stay on securely.

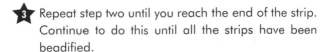 Repeat step two until you reach the end of the strip. Continue to do this until all the strips have been beadified.

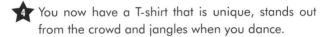 You now have a T-shirt that is unique, stands out from the crowd and jangles when you dance.

DID YOU KNOW?

Unlike the extortionate prices we are used to paying for festival tickets, the three-day Rock al Parque festival in Colombia does not charge an admission fee. Not surprisingly, the festival attracts an estimated 88,600 visitors a day.

TOP TIP

GAFFA WHAT?!

As mentioned before, kebab-munching, beer-slurping giants will almost certainly be slumping on a tent near you. So might the hyperactive spritely danceaholics and the easy-going average Joes, too. To help you be prepared for the damage that might be caused by someone visualising themselves as one of the backing dancers from the night's performance, arm yourself with a roll of gaffa tape. If you do wake up in the morning to a collapsing tent, you can easily fix any broken poles by wrapping the damaged parts up with the strong stuff.

≈ FESTIVAL FAUX PAS ≈

YOU CAN LEAVE YOUR PANTS ON

Seeing the horror on someone's face as they witness someone just a stone's throw away flashing their milky white boobs or shrivelled scrotum is priceless; however, that memory could scar them for the rest of their life. The cause isn't worth the effect. A lot of dignity will be lost at some point or other during the festival, but for the sake of others, try to keep everything strapped in securely.

MUSIC PRODUCES
A KIND OF PLEASURE
which human nature
CANNOT DO
WITHOUT.

★ *Confucius* ★

★ FESTIVAL HACK ★

To help conserve your phone battery, whenever you're not using it switch it to airplane mode. Allocate a certain number of times to look at your phone per day and get all your texts and phone calls out of the way in one go so that you can go back to enjoying your time at the festival without any interruption.

TOP TIP

GADGET ENVY

When you are away from your tent make sure that you take all your valuables with you and keep them close so you know where they are. Alternatively, most festivals provide lockers for you to put your things in when you don't need them. I would advise doing this so that you can feel at ease and enjoy your festival experience to the fullest.

However, if you are considering taking some sort of gadget that you have worked hard to save for but isn't essential, leave it at home where it's safe. The more items of worth that you are seen to be carrying, the more likely you will be pinpointed as a good target.

There is no religion BUT SEX AND MUSIC.

★ *Sting* ★

≈ FESTIVAL FAUX PAS ≈

FLY ME TO THE STAGE

Never link arms with your friends as a tactic to push the crowd out of the way to get you nearer the stage. You WILL be punished – either at the festival, at an unlikely moment later in your pitiful life or in your afterlife. The first is the most likely.

TOP TIP

THE FESTIVALLER AT NIGHT-TIME

With people partying into the early hours of the morning it's unlikely that you will feel unsafe. However, with a bit of Dutch courage (and often chemical courage) firing the minds and bodies of other festivallers, it is difficult to gauge how and when a situation could develop. To prevent feeling isolated and being an easy target when you are walking back to your tent at night, make sure, when possible, that you stick with at least one other person and keep to lit walkways. If there is trouble brewing then it's always best, no matter how nosy you are, to keep your head down and keep walking.

WHERE WORDS
LEAVE OFF,
MUSIC BEGINS.

★ *Heinrich Heine* ★

WORST FESTIVAL MOMENT

Dubbed a shambles by festival goers, the Z008 festival in Kent has become known as one of the biggest flops in the Biggest Festival Flops Hall of Infamy. The complaints were louder than the music and the event was doomed from the start. The arrival queues were too long, the campsite was overcrowded, finding drinkable water was like finding a needle in a haystack and the line-up and schedule mess-ups were almost as frequent as Beyoncé's outfit changes. I was wary of it as soon as I knew the twist was 'music meets mammal'. Drunk dancing and lions is not a favourable mix.

TOP TIP

SUN CREAM, NOT SUN SCREAM

You don't want to ruin your festival experience by getting sunburnt – sunstroke is not fun, especially when you're sleeping in a hot tent and it's noisy. Even if you are good at applying sun cream you can still get sunburnt when you are outside all day. Here are some tips for staying safe in the sun that you might not have thought about before:

Don't apply the cream too thinly – although sun cream is mega expensive and you want it to last as long as possible, you aren't going to be protected by putting on a few blobs. Experts say that for each application, you should be using a fifth of a 200-ml bottle.

It's pretty difficult to do this in reality, but if you can, try to stay in the shade for part of the peak of the day (between noon and 2 p.m.). Even if it's just for an hour, it'll still help decrease your chances of getting sunburnt.

If you're going to wear sun cream, wear it properly and make sure you apply it more than once, even if you've got the all-day stuff. It's very easy to forget to do this when you're having such a good time, so it might be worth setting a time with your friends for you all to reapply it. At least then there are more chances of someone remembering.

To make applying sun cream as easy a task as possible, buy the spray-on cream. It's hassle-free and you won't have to put up with sticky hands for the rest of the day.

Bring some lip salve with you! You don't want your lips burning – think about all the drink that you won't be able to enjoy.

★ FASHION ME FESTIVAL ★

OUT OF SIGHT, OUT OF MIND

If your hair turns into a grease ball immediately after you've washed it, like mine does, by the second or third day of being at the festival, your luscious locks will have probably malformed into lank bits of lard, and your patience to try to do anything with them will be diminishing. Like the good old adage 'out of sight, out of mind', you'll be wishing you hair was someplace hidden from your vision. If you have long locks, here are a few hairstyles to help you forget about your mop and leave the dry shampoo at home:

The Messy French Twist:

 To create the messy look, lightly comb your hair back, using your fingers, as if you were about to tie it up in a mid-ponytail.

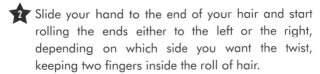 Slide your hand to the end of your hair and start rolling the ends either to the left or the right, depending on which side you want the twist, keeping two fingers inside the roll of hair.

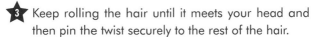 Keep rolling the hair until it meets your head and then pin the twist securely to the rest of the hair.

 Spray liberally with hairspray.

The Milkmaid Braid:

Brush your hair so that there aren't any tangles and part it in the middle.

Plait both sections of your hair so that they start just above each ear. Tie them at the ends with a band.

Take one of the plaits and position it just after the start of your hairline. Secure it in place using hair grips.

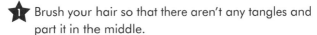 Then take the other plait and place it on top of the pinned plait. Feed the unplaited end section of the plait on top underneath the other. Grip it in place so that the hair pins aren't visible.

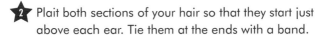 Spray liberally with hairspray.

The Wrapped Ponytail:

 Comb your hair lightly using your fingertips and tie it up in a ponytail.

 Separate a piece of hair from the bottom of the ponytail, about as thick as a pencil, and twist it round the hairband.

 Once the end of the piece of hair is back round at the bottom of the ponytail, tuck it into the hairband. Use hair grips for extra hold.

The Fishtail:

Easy to do, this style disguises greasy hair and could even help you in the event of heavy floods (well, that's if you take the name literally). Here are the steps to get the stylish fishtail look:

1 Part your hair in a side parting and place your hair over the shoulder on the opposite side to where the parting is.

2 Split your hair in two equal sections, still keeping it to the side.

3 Take a small piece of hair from the outside of one of the sections of hair and move it to the inside of the other section.

4 Take an equal piece of hair from the other section and repeat the step you have just performed.

5 Pull both sections tight and you'll see a cross.

6 Repeat steps 3, 4 and 5 in order until you reach the end and tie it with a hairband.

7 If you want to achieve the messy look, tug at a few pieces of hair in the plait, although it's pretty certain that in a few hours that look will just come naturally.

If all else fails, remember to pack some dry shampoo!

MUSIC?

MUSIC IS LIFE!

It's physical emotion –

YOU CAN TOUCH IT!

★ *Isaac Marion* ★

ONE BANANA, TWO BANANA, THREE BANANA, FOUR

Although it's not wise to stock up on perishable and easy-to-bruise fresh foods, a bunch of bananas could do you the world of good when you're feeling a bit groggy. For one, they are gentle on the stomach and therefore less likely to make an unwanted reappearance. They are also good for boosting your blood sugar, something that's necessary after last night's booze binge has left you feeling lifeless. Another thing that we lose as we consume more alcohol, leading to the feeling of dehydration, is potassium, which is another slice of goodness found aplenty in bananas.

★ FESTIVAL HACK ★

There's nothing better than having a BBQ with your friends on your first festival evening. But if there isn't an experienced fire starter among you, you could be starved of the sausages that are waiting to be cooked. Thankfully, that's where this hack comes in useful.

Instead of taking a big bag of charcoal with you, pack each piece of charcoal individually in the compartments of a 12- or 18-hole cardboard egg box. Not only will this save you lugging a heavy bag of charcoal round, the egg container also acts as an easy-to-start fire pack. All you have to do is light the egg container and the fire will catch onto the charcoal. Happy barbequing – and make sure you roast some Starburst sweets for dessert – delicious!

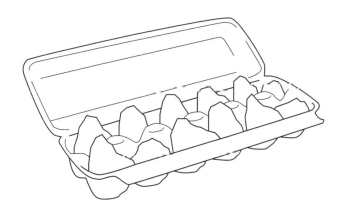

≈ FESTIVAL FAUX PAS ≈

THE LONG AND WINDING QUEUE

Queuing comes naturally to most well-mannered people, so why does our etiquette go out the window as soon as someone gives us a tent, a few beers and some music? Yes, we know that you are pretty close to wetting yourself or passing out from dehydration – we all are – but it doesn't make you exempt from joining the queue.

THE LEGACY YOU
LEAVE BEHIND
IS THE MUSIC.

★ *Serge Pizzorno* ★

TOP TIP

THERE'S A THIEF IN MY TENT

For most people who attend festivals, the experience is a whirlwind of fun and memorable moments. But although it's no good to worry incessantly about things like security and your valuables, it is beneficial to keep in mind some ways of decreasing your chances of having a bad experience:

Although it seems like the logical thing to do, don't lock up your tent when you leave it. It'll only invite thieves to think that you have valuables stored inside. A lock isn't going to stop them tearing through the flimsy material of the tent.

There could be a very small possibility that thieves will try to steal things from your tent while you are sleeping. To beat them at their own game, the best place to stash your valuables is in the bottom of your sleeping bag. The thing that then lies between the thief and the valuables is you, sleeping soundly and holding the fort without even knowing it.

If the above does happen, and you wake up from slumber, do your best to restrain yourself from confronting or challenging an intruder. Instead, wait until they have departed the area and then go and tell festival staff or the police. In the moment you may want to give them what they deserve, but it'll only provoke them more.

PLAY IT F**KIN' LOUD!

★ *Bob Dylan* ★

★ FESTIVAL HACK ★

Taking matches to a festival is pretty essential for all sorts of miscellaneous situations. However, the strike pads on 'strike anywhere' matchboxes can be a bit temperamental. To ensure you don't have to do the rounds of your neighbours, asking if you can borrow their strike pads, take a strip of sandpaper – or a nail file if you want your luggage to be as multifunctional as possible!

TOP TIP

LET'S PRETEND THIS NEVER HAPPENED

OK, so here's the moment where an elephant turns up out of the blue and a tumbleweed rolls across the floor in front of where you are sitting. Yes, I'm going to sound like your mother, but let's just view this as a form of preparation for the conversation she will have with you that is almost inevitable and very likely imminent.

If you happen to meet someone and sneak off with them to discuss your limitless similarities in terms of music, politics and philosophy (and do other things almost as riveting), make sure those things are done a) discreetly – even though the third person in the tent with you is apparently 'sleeping', the likelihood is that they are awake/ going to be woken and will have to suffer through the whole shebang, thus ruining their festival time and maybe even their life – and b) with a condom. Also, if they ask to go to an area of the campsite you aren't familiar with, make sure you don't go with 'the good idea they've just had'. OK, I've said my piece – now go and have fun.

DID YOU KNOW?

Sziget Festival in Budapest, dubbed The Island of Freedom, is a whole festival world of its own. Located on its own separate island, the festival boasts non-stop events in over 50 venues. These include live concerts, ongoing parties and theatre and circus exhibitions. And with 400,000 attendees from over 70 countries across the globe, a vast amount of space is obviously a requirement!

WITHOUT MUSIC,
life would be 🏕
A MISTAKE.

★ *Friedrich Nietzsche* ★

≈ FESTIVAL FAUX PAS ≈

SOCIAL MEDIA WILL TEAR US APART

You're at a festival, in the middle of a huge crowd watching a well-loved band playing your favourite song, and all you can do is tweet about it… really?! You may get a few favourites, maybe even a couple of retweets, but to sacrifice an unforgettable memory – is it really worth it? Stop writing about it and start living it.

BEST FESTIVAL MOMENT

As more and more festivals are popping up across the globe, festival organisers are thinking of ways to make their festival unique. Nowadays festivals aren't just about the music and camping, as we are often offered some other memorable experience as well, such as the mud wrestling, paint fights and dance-offs at the Secret Garden Party in Cambridgeshire. Check out their 2012 paint fight on YouTube – a spectrum of pure colourful delight!

FASHION ME FESTIVAL

PRICELESS PONCHO

As rain usually announces itself as the main headline in the line-up of forecast predictions, here's a DIY idea that will ensure you stay (almost) dry and have fun even in the wettest of weather.

What you need: plastic shower curtain, clear nylon thread, tissue paper, leather needle, your mum's sewing machine, permanent marker.

 Replace the regular needle on the sewing machine with a needle for stitching leather. Thread the bobbin with nylon thread and set the stitch length to three or higher. Remember when you start sewing through the plastic to place a layer of tissue paper underneath it to prevent the plastic from sticking to the machine.

 If you're taking the shower curtain from your bathroom, remove the hooks and clean it thoroughly to remove mildew. If it's brand new this step isn't necessary. Either way, make sure that the shower curtain has a jazzy pattern, or else is see-through if you want to have a go at decorating it yourself.

 Cut the shower curtain to 55 in wide, keeping the existing length. Cut away the seams, such as the one at the top of the curtain. Draw a 12 in line parallel to the bottom of the shower curtain, exactly in the middle and cut along it. This will be the hole for your head.

 Take the excess piece of shower curtain and fold it in half. Draw a shape that resembles an outline of half a human head and neck, starting at the fold, and cut it out. Sew a seam along the edge of the curves to join them together.

 Find the centre of the 12 in line you cut in step three. Cut a 2-in slit in the middle of the horizontal slit and pin the flaps back. Pin the hood you made in step 4 underneath the two flaps.

 Sew all the way round the neck hole, where the hood meets the cloak, to prevent rain seeping in and to stop the plastic from splitting. There you have your DIY poncho, ready for pimping to your heart's content.

⭐ **7** If you don't have the patience or a penchant for craft, you can always go to a local supermarket and purchase a Pac-A-Mac – a cheap alternative that is easy to pack and suitable for all your wet-weather needs.

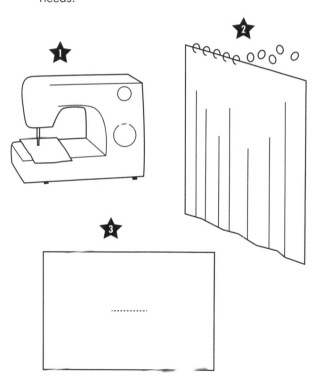

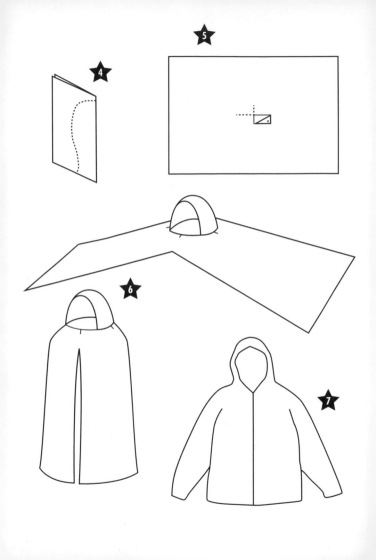

★ FESTIVAL HACK ★

It's dark, you peaked long ago and all you want to do is get some sleep. You've found your way back to the tent, but getting into it is another story as you keep tripping up on the tent's ropes.

This hack will help to reduce your chances of tripping on the ropes and causing an accident, as well as enabling you to find that elusive tent entrance more easily. Take a pool noodle and cut it to the length of the ropes – a brightly coloured one will make your tent easier to identify. Then make a vertical slit down one side and into the middle of the pool noodle with a penknife. Now, once you've pitched your tent you can latch the foam pieces around the ropes. If you want extra visibility, try decorating the pool noodles with glow-in-the-dark paint.

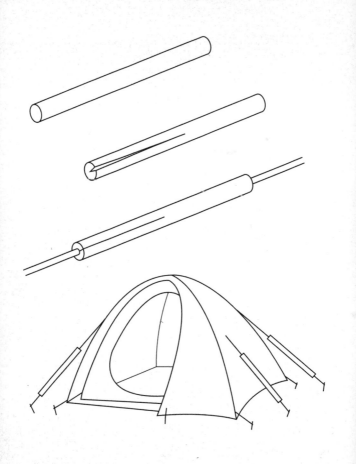

EVERYBODY AND EVERYTHING IS MUSIC.

★ *Jimi Hendrix* ★

If you're interested in finding out more
about our books, find us on Facebook at
Summersdale Publishers and follow us
on Twitter at **@Summersdale**.

www.summersdale.com